WHAT'S THIS BOOK F

This book provides very short p
EMERGENCY briefing just before curtain-up. There's also a hint as to how the action starts...

WHERE ARE WE?   WHO ARE THESE CHARACTERS?
WHAT IS GOING ON?

It is aimed at those who have not had time to assimilate a normal synopsis and/or who find plots difficult - and this includes both novices and quite a few experienced opera-goers as well.

It is also useful as a quick reference book.

However one must be wary, because shortening the summary can distort some plots and remove interesting sub-plots as well as quite a few fascinating characters. Of course some operas can be summarised more successfully than others.

Here I have experimented with shorter and longer summaries and included compromises that give reasonable intelligibility without too much distortion.

The original challenge was to get each plot into three sentences - but I have found it advisable to break the rule rather often. I even attempted newspaper headline summaries, but these were more amusing than informative - you may wish to make up your own!

Ideally you should be able to follow an opera by hearing the words and understanding the action *as it happens*, but this is rarely possible. Surtitles help but are not the full answer - and the solution generally adopted is to struggle with reading a more detailed plot synopsis (or better still a full libretto) before a performance.

"Kobbé" is the standard reference but everyone has different preferences. I like the much shorter summaries in the *Rough Guide to Opera* (Matthew Boyden) and the *New Penguin Opera Guide* (Amanda Holden), whilst the *"101 Opera Librettos"* published by Black Dog and Leventhal (ed. Konemann) enable you to read every word. Stephen Williams has a very relaxed style in his "*Come to the Opera*", probably out of print. However be warned: Kobbé is about 4lb in weight and the 101 weighs in even heavier.

WHICH OPERAS?

I've made a personal selection of commonly performed operas plus a few border-line or unfashionable ones; a grand total of 119. I've put them alphabetically using the English or foreign names that seem commonest, with cross references where necessary. I'm not a stickler for consistency or correct accents in every case.

At the end I have put an essay on some practical aspects of opera-going on the assumption that most of my readers will be fairly new to opera.

This is the sort of book that gets refined and added to, and if you would like to participate with helpful comments (and get a mention) please do.

POTTED OPERA PLOTS

By Martin Funnell

Written and set by
author Martin Funnell
© Martin Funnell 2004
ISBN 1-902658-16-7
All rights reserved.
Published by Vineyard Hill
(2005 revision)

AIDA

Verdi - 1871 – set in Egypt during war with Ethiopia.

Following the Egyptian conquest of Ethiopia, Aida, daughter of Amonastro (King of Ethiopia) is made a slave to Amneris, daughter of the Egyptian King, and both are in love with Radames, Captain of the Egyptian guard. He is in love with Aida and rejects Amneris.

Amonasro, a captive of the Egyptians, persuades Aida to extract military secrets from Radames, but as she is doing so they are discovered. He is sentenced to death by "entombment" and Aida joins him.

Starts with Ramphis the High Priest meeting Radames in the Egyptian King's palace…

[Celebrated triumphal procession in Act 2].

AKHNATEN

Glass - 1984 - Egypt, 1370 BC

Akhnaten becomes ruler of Egypt and, prompted by the previous ruler's wife Queen Tye, discards the old religions, sacks the priests and destroys the temples, creating a new city Akhetaten and acquiring a beautiful Queen (Nefertiti).

At the moment when hostile invaders approach the priests regain control - and Akhnaten disappears mysteriously. Tourists now wander among the ruins, but life on the Nile continues as it always has done.

Starts with a stage loaded with sand and Egyptians…

ALBERT HERRING

Britten - 1947 - set in East Suffolk town 1900

In order to show up the appalling morals of the town girls, imperious Lady Billows gets innocent Albert made "May King".

Mischievous friends Sid and Nancy get him drunk at the civic celebrations, and he disappears overnight to reappear later next day - somewhat dishevelled - as all are mourning his death.

Starts with housekeeper fussing in Lady Billows' breakfast room before the arrival of the Vicar, Mayor, and the Superintendent of Police...

ALCESTE

Gluck - 1767 - Greek gods

King Admetus is ill and the oracle says that he must die unless another can die instead of him.

His wife offers herself but Admetus refuses to accept her sacrifice and they both die. Hercules and Apollo rescue them both from hell.

Starts with the crowd (and later Queen Alcestis) in front of the palace mourning the illness of the King...

ALCINA

Handel - 1735 - set on enchanted island

Enchantress Alcina holds Knight Ruggiero in thrall. His betrothed (Bradamante) tries to release him but does not succeed until an urn containing Alcina's magic gets smashed.

Starts with Bradamante and her guardian being discovered by Alcina's sister and led off to see Alcina...

ANDREA CHÉNIER

Giordano - 1896 - set in 18C France

Maddalena loves poet Chenier and his left-wing political writings. But being an aristocrat during the Revolution means she has to hide to save her life.

When attempting to protect her, Chenier injures the servant, Gerard (a revolutionary) and is arrested, so she emerges and joins him in prison to await death.

Starts with preparations for a big party and Gerard mocking aristocratic life - then the Countess comes in to supervise things...

ARABELLA

Richard Strauss 1933   set in Vienna hotel 1860

Arabella's impoverished parents want to marry their beautiful daughter to a rich suitor to improve their fortunes, but she is indifferent to all her suitors, even Matteo who is wildly in love with her.

Arabella's sister Zdenka has been brought up as a boy to save money but has fallen for Matteo, and writes him love letters purporting to be from Arabella.

At a ball Arabella meets Mandryka and they fall in love.

Zdenka tricks Matteo into her bedroom instead of Arabella's and we get a sequence of misunderstandings climaxing with satisfactory pairing off and happiness.

Starts with parents consulting a fortune-teller and complaining of poverty...

ARIADNE ON NAXOS

Richard Strauss – 1912- Classical Greek opera played inside Viennese Mansion, 19C

A patron has required simultaneous performances of an opera and a harlequinade, to be followed by fireworks.

There is a chaotic *Prologue* in which a serious opera composer and actors prepare for a rather mixed entertainment.

In the *Opera* proper we see forsaken Ariadne in suicidal despair being comforted (unsuccessfully) by her nymphs, and again later by harlequinade character effervescent Zerbinetta. Then boozy god Bacchus arrives steamy for love, and Ariadne is reassured in a fairly happy ending.

Starts with a chaotic scene of preparations for the performances.

[This is the second version, the original had an operatic piece following a version of "Le Bourgeois Gentilhomme" by Moliere].

UN BALLO IN MASCHERA
– ["A Masked Ball", pg 44].

THE BARBER OF SEVILLE

Rossini - 1816 - set in 18C Spain

Figaro (a resourceful Barber) helps Count Almaviva to woo Rosina, who is the pretty ward of stuffy old Don Basilio. Basilio is however quite keen to marry her himself.

He is outwitted after a sequence of events including (a) the Count pretending to be a soldier to get billeted in Don Basilio's house, (b) the Count taking on the role of Rosina's singing teacher, (c) an attempted elopement, (d) Basilio's misuse of a love letter.

Starts with Count Almaviva serenading Rosina outside Dr Bartolo's house...

THE BARTERED BRIDE

Smetana - 1866 - set in 19C Czech village.

The fortunes of lovers Jenik and Marenka undergo many reverses in this romp of village life. Marenka is told to marry stammering Vasek on the assumption that he is the first son of rich Micha - but in the end he turns out to be the second, so she gets preferred lover and inheritance.

There are complications including a voluble marriage broker and Vasek impersonating a bear.

Starts with jollity outside the village inn, with our two lovers looking sad because Marenka has just learnt that she cannot marry Jenik...

THE BEGGAR'S OPERA

Gay - 1728 - set in early 18C London

Set amongst the criminal fraternity (Ladies of the town and Gentlemen of the road), highwayman Macheath enjoys women, drink and crime but is about to be executed.

Polly (a fence's daughter) and Lucy (a gaoler's daughter) and four other criminal wives of Macheath are involved in complicated goings-on. He just about survives.

Starts with a Prologue and then the fence Peachum doing his accounts as his gang drop in to discuss crime...

BILLY BUDD

Britten -1951- set on board HMS Indomitable, 1797

In a navy scared rigid by the earliest signs of possible mutiny against harsh conditions, innocent young Able Seaman Billy Budd thinks the sea is "the life for him".

His goodness touches a raw nerve in evil Master-of-Arms Claggart, who plots against him, eventually provoking Billy to strike and accidentally kill him. Billy calmly accepts his sentence of death, and idealistic Captain Vere regrets all - whilst the music seems to offer hope.

Starts with Captain Vere reminiscing, and then the men appear working on deck, revealing the harsh discipline in force at the time... [All male].

LA BOHÈME

Puccini - 1896 - set in Bohemian Paris

Penurious young poet Rudolph and embroiderer Mimi fall passionately in love in a cold garret. They are surrounded by penniless and easy-going friends (Musetta and Marcello are among them) but Mimi's fickleness and his jealousy poison the relationship. Mimi falls sick and everyone rallies round, and as she dies their passionate love is briefly rekindled.

Starts in the attic studio shared by Rudolph and 3 friends gazing out at the roofs under frost...

BORIS GODOUNOV

Mussorgsky - 1874 - set in Russia

Boris is crowned Tsar in style, but has a guilty secret - he had the Tsar's younger son murdered in childhood. Grigory, pretender to the tsardom, disguised as a monk, decides to bring Boris to justice, and so Boris tries to capture him. Boris has agonies of remorse and eventually dies on the throne.

Starts in monastery courtyard with police haranguing a crowd to make them persuade Boris to accept the crown...

LA CALISTO

Cavalli - 1651 - set in mythical Arcadia

One of Diana's beautiful nymphs, Calisto, has caught the eye of Jove, who tries to seduce her - but she repulses him. So Jove disguises himself as Diana and succeeds. However Jove's jealous wife Juno then gets the Furies to turn Calisto into a bear, but ever resourceful Jove makes her immortal by turning her into Ursa Major.

In a sub-plot the real Diana falls for shepherd-boy Endymion but cannot return his love because of her vows of chastity. Her passion is discovered by jealous Pan, and Endymion is punished. They agree to stop at just kissing.

Starts with a prologue in which Nature and Eternity celebrate mortals who are now immortal - like Calisto.

CANDIDE
Bernstein – 1957

This version of a Voltaire play starts with Voltaire himself and Candide, the illegitimate son of a Baron's sister, living happily in a Westphalia castle. Voltaire takes the part of Pangloss who preaches OPTIMISM whilst both characters undergo the most degrading experiences before escaping to the new world - which inspires yet more OPTIMISM.

More degrading experiences follow (Act 2) in South America and Pangloss finally gives up OPTIMISM in favour of WORK without any philosophy at all except to make his garden grow as Candide recommends.

Starts with Voltaire, joined by the complete cast as he starts to tell his story...

[Several versions, and you might classify it as a play].

CARMEN
Bizet - 1875 - set in 1820's Spain.

Sexy gipsy Carmen goes to prison for quarrelling but gets herself out by seducing a guard, Don Jose, who is punished. She seduces him again thus ruining him completely - but not quenching his ardour for her. He joins some smugglers and fights off a rival (Escamillo) but Carmen no longer fancies him, and when he returns (from a brief visit to his dying mother) she repulses him - and in a passion he kills her.

Starts in a square in Seville with brightly dressed ladies and red coated dragoons - and a bell signals noon and cigarette factory girls enter...

CAVALLERIA RUSTICANA

Mascagni - 1890 - set in Sicily

Handsome ex-soldier Turiddu has got bored with his mistress (Santuzza). He takes over a former lover (Lola) who has married in the meantime. Santuzza tells Lola's husband, and he kills Turiddu.

Starts in village square with Easter crowds..

(Short opera usually done with "I Pagliacci" and often shortened to "Cav")

LA CENERENTOLA *see "Cinderella" below*

CINDERELLA *Rossini - 1817 - set in 18C Italy*

The Prince and his Valet are induced by a playful tutor to dress up as each other. When visiting the Don Magnifico mansion the Prince thus charms pretty Cinderella in her kitchen whilst the valet flatters the Ugly Sisters.

Whilst the Prince is happy to agree marriage when Cinderella appears at court, she insists on him finding her by locating a bracelet - which his tutor contrives to make happen.

Starts with Cinderella making coffee for her ugly sisters before the Prince's friend enters disguised as a beggar...

LA CLEMENZA DI TITO

Mozart - 1791 - set in Rome 79-81 AD

Emperor Titus first plans to marry his mistress, Berenice, but Rome will not allow this so he turns to Servilia, sister of his close friend Sextus.

Sextus loves the ambitious Vitellia, now spurned a second time by Titus; she plots revenge and tells Sextus that she will marry him if he will kill Titus.

When Servilia tells Titus she is engaged to Sextus's friend Annius, Titus changes his mind again and decides to marry Vitellia after all - but too late to stop the plot.

The Capitol is burnt and there is general mourning for Titus, but he survives – the wrong man was killed. Sextus is arrested and Vitellia confesses he did it for love of her.

Titus displays his famous clemency and pardons everyone.

Starts with Vitellia revealing Titus's plan to marry Berenice and urging Sextus to assassinate him...

LE COMTE ORY

Rossini - 1828 - set in Touraine, time of Crusades

Philandering Comte Ory and his companions make several comic attempts to seduce the Countess Adele and her ladies in the castle while her husband is away at the Crusades, but the ladies have vowed chastity and Ory is frustrated every time.

A first attempt in hermit disguise to "absolve" them from their inconvenient vows is followed by Isolier (Ory's page who is in love with Adele) trying to enter the castle as a pilgrim with Ory and his gang. They finally succeed disguised as nuns "escaping from Ory". As matters begin to get out of hand it is reported that the Crusaders are returning...

Starts with Ory's friend Raimbaud (disguised) summoning the peasantry to give alms to the "Hermit", to be followed by Adele's companion seeking the hermit's advice...

THE CORONATION OF POPPEA

Monteverdi - 1642 - set in Rome

Emperor Nero abandons his wife Octavia in favour of sexy Poppea. His wise counsellor Seneca criticises his action so is honour bound to kill himself. Former lover Ottone plots Poppea's death but is forestalled - love and ambition triumph and Nero is joined with Poppea.

Starts with guards outside Poppea's house and Ottone slowly realising that Nero is inside with her...

COSI FAN TUTTE

Mozart - 1790 - set in 18C Naples

A moral/comic opera about the unfaithfulness of women which starts and ends with two happy couples. For a bet the two men agree to dress up as sexy Albanians and test the fidelity of their lovers by attempting to seduce each other's partner. The ladies prove unfaithful, but their marriages to the "Albanians" are aborted when all is revealed.

Starts with the men in a cafe discussing the fidelity of their lovers with a third...

THE CUNNING LITTLE VIXEN

Janacek - 1924 - set in Czech countryside.

A Forester catches a vixen as a pet, but she gets bored, kills some chickens and escapes, making a new home in a badger's sett. In the woods and village animals and humans discuss life and the future, and the vixen meets a mate. Later on a poacher Harasta is taunted by the vixen and kills her. But the Forester finds one of her cubs - and muses about "life always beginning all over again".

Starts in the woods with animals, badger (smoking) and dragonfly - then the Forester enters for a nap...

DIDO AND AENEAS

Purcell - 1689 - set in ancient Greece

Dido (Queen of Carthage) and warrior Aeneas are in love, but a sorceress, determined to destroy them both, sends her spirit to appear to Aeneas as Mercury, commanding Aeneas to fulfil his destiny and found Troy. He departs and a despairing Dido kills herself.

Starts with Dido at home being cheered up by her companion (Belinda) before she bemoans her fate...

DON CARLOS

Verdi - 1867 - set in 16C France and Spain.

Don Carlos (King's son) and his arranged bride Elisabeth are in love, but then the King marries her himself.

Impetuous Carlos rashly draws his sword in front of the King, and the Inquisitor rules he must be killed. Elisabeth is shown to retain affection for Carlos and is also disgraced, but in the last scene Don Carlos is saved by his grandfather's ghost.

Starts with a hunting scene where Elisabeth loses her page and goes off, whilst Carlos enters, sings of his love for her just before she returns and they meet. He is in disguise - but is soon recognised and they fall in love..

DON GIOVANNI

Mozart - 1787 - set in 17C Spain

Libertine Don Giovanni (accompanied by comic servant Leporello) is caught seducing the daughter (Anna) of the Commendatore, and kills the latter in a fracas. He avoids an abandoned admirer (Elvira) turning his attentions to Zerlina. She turns out to be well guarded by her fiancé Masetto who, with some peasants, instigates a manhunt for Don Giovanni. After many adventures Don Giovanni invites the Commendatore's statue to dinner and is dragged down to hell.

Starts with Leporello lurking in someone's garden complaining about being a servant to Don Giovanni - who is nearby seducing a lady...

DON PASQUALE

Donizetti - 1843 - set in 19C Europe

Wealthy old Don Pasquale fancies young Norina, but so does his more suitable nephew Ernesto.

Friend-of-the-family Dr Malatesta arranges to trick Don Pasquale into a mock marriage, making sure Norina will behave so badly that he will abandon his romantic notions for ever. He is only too glad to let Norina marry Ernesto.

Starts with Don Pasquale in his room impatiently awaiting Dr Malatesta…

DUKE BLUEBEARD'S CASTLE

Bartok - 1918 – Legendary

Duke Bluebeard's wife Judith pleads to be shown inside the seven doors of his castle in turn and is shocked to see his past life and previous three wives.

Having opened the doors despite his warnings she then has to go through the last and join his other wives.

Bluebeard is alone again.

Starts with Bluebeard leading Judith into a round room in his castle with seven closed doors...

ELEKTRA

Richard Strauss – 1909 - in Palace of Mycenae, BC

Elektra is seething with anger because her mother, Queen Klytemnestra has murdered her father, King Agamemnon and installed lover Aegisthus in his place. To make matters worse Klytemnestra has demoted Elektra and sent her brother Orestes away - so we soon see Elektra planning to kill her mother.

However, after spreading news that he is dead, Orestes returns secretly, revealing himself to Elektra. He kills Klytemnestra, and Aegisthus and Elektra die soon after.

Starts with servants despising Elektra, who is forced to live with the dogs...

L'ELISIR D'AMORE (Elixir of Love)

Donizetti - 1832 - set in 19C Italian village.

Adina spurns the feeble approaches of shy Nemorino and wonders if he will ever ask her to marry him. Much teased, he strengthens his resolve with some rather alcoholic "elixir d'amour" pushed by a convenient quack, becomes drunk and then strangely indifferent to Adina. Emboldened by the "elixir", Nemorino enlists in order to pay for more, but suddenly inherits a fortune and is shrewdly bought out of the army by Adina...who finishes up in his arms (and the "elixir" makes a fortune for the quack).

Starts on Adina's farm with Nemorino singing of her beauty and Adina responding negatively...

EUGENE ONEGIN

Tchaikovsky - 1879 - set in 19C Russia

Onegin insensitively rebuffs young Tatiana (who has fallen for him) and flirts with her sister, who is already engaged to a friend. Onegin kills her lover in a duel thus losing the friend. Years later he meets Tatiana again, now the wife of Prince Gremin. Onegin falls in love with her and pleads with her to abandon Gremin, but she refuses and leaves him distraught.

Starts in Mme Larina's garden as she recalls the old days, whilst her daughters look forward..

EURYANTHE

Weber - 1823 - set in 12C France

Count Lysiart bets his all that he can seduce Euryanthe from her betrothed Count Adolar. Eglantine (who also loves Adolar) discredits Euryanthe so that Adolar loses his woman, bet and possessions - and, in despair, he departs to the mountains. But when he reappears at the wedding of Lysiart and Eglantine all is revealed - with murder and mayhem. Adolar gets Euryanthe in the end.

Starts in Count Adolar's palace where he chants the beauty of his betrothed Euryanthe to Count Lysiart...

FALSTAFF

Verdi - 1893 - set in 17C Windsor

Falstaff is a jovial stout old knight with a taste for drink and seduction. He fancies two "Merry Wives" (Page and Ford), but they are fully aware of his intentions and catch him and pitch him into the Thames in a laundry basket.

Later he is trapped into an assignation in Windsor forest at midnight and is humiliated by the same ladies and townsfolk dressed as fairies. He shrugs it off as a joke.

Starts at Garter Inn with Dr Caius complaining about Falstaff...

[Same story as "The Merry Wives of Windsor"]

FAUST

Gounod - 1859 - set in Europe

Faust bargains with the Devil (Mephistopheles) for the return of his youth, and then seduces innocent young Marguerite, who has a child.

Her brother attempts to avenge her disgrace but is killed by Faust aided by Mephistopheles, thus driving Marguerite insane. She kills her child.

Mephistopheles now comes to take Faust to hell, but Marguerite won't follow him - she goes instead to heaven.

Starts with Faust feeling old, and cursing God. Mephistopheles appears with a proposal...

LA FEDELTA PREMIATA

Haydn - 1781 - set in mythical times

To fulfil a curse, two faithful lovers have to be sacrificed to a monster each year. Luckily for the current pair (Fileno and Celia) the monster transforms into Diana at the crucial moment and absolves them, removing the curse for ever.

Starts with Nymphs and Shepherds in front of Diana's temple begging her to relent...

FIDELIO

Beethoven - 1805 - Set in 18C Spanish fortress

Don Pizarro, a wicked prison governor has incarcerated Florestan and announced that he is dead, but Florestan's wife Leonora thinks he is alive and gets a job disguised as a male warder called Fidelio to find him.

The prison is to be inspected shortly so, to maintain the governor's story, Florestan must be killed. Rocco, the jailor, tells Leonora to dig a grave in readiness, but she recognises Florestan and manages to stop his murder just as the Minister of State arrives - so all is revealed, the governor disgraced and the couple reunited.

Starts with the jailor's assistant discussing marriage with Rocco's daughter - but she really loves Fidelio...

DIE FLEDERMAUS

Johann Strauss - 1874 - set in 19C Vienna.

Set in a decadent capital where everyone seems intent on infidelity this opera scandalised many. A complicated plot is stirred up by a Dr Falke, taking revenge on Eisenstein for having embarrassed him when in bat fancy dress. Lured to a masked ball, Eisenstein attempts flirtation with his wife Roselinda, and her lover Alfred is mistakenly sent to prison instead of Eisenstein. Other characters, in or out of disguise, complicate matters even more, but all ends well.

Starts inside Rosalinda's house. Her lover (Alfred) is heard serenading her off stage and her maid enters...

THE FLYING DUTCHMAN (Fliegende Hollander)

Wagner - 1843 - set in 18C Norway

A Dutch captain is destined to sail eternally for seven year stretches until he is redeemed by the love of a faithful woman. A local seaman introduces his daughter (Senta) to the captain and they fall in love, but confused by the overheard protestations of a hunter who is in love with her the captain abandons her, going off on another seven year voyage. Senta is so upset she casts herself off a rock, proving her love for him and thus saving him.

Starts with a storm at sea and sailors...

THE FORCE OF DESTINY

Verdi - 1862-9 - set in mediaeval Spain

Don Alvaro attempts to elope with Leonora but is thwarted by her father the Marquis who gets killed accidentally in a fracas leaving Leonora to seek refuge in a hermit's cell.

Her brother Don Carlo determines to avenge the death, but makes a friendship pact with Don Alvaro after battlefield incidents when neither knows who the other is. When Don Carlo discovers the truth they duel and Don Alvaro has to retire to a monastery; but Don Carlo seeks him out and they fight again - but Alvaro wounds Carlo who, as he dies, kills Leonora in revenge.

Starts with Leonora's father saying goodnight; then she gets remorseful about her impending elopement...

DER FREISCHÜTZ

Weber - 1821 - set in 17C Bohemia

Max loves Agatha who is to be the prize at a shooting match. Evil Kaspar lures Max into a haunted glen where he makes him some magic bullets, the last of which can be specially directed.

At the contest the last bullet kills Kaspar and in consequence Max is put on probation - but with the prospect of acquiring Agatha at the end of it.

Starts as a peasant has just defeated the forester Max at a shooting match...

GIANNI SCHICCHI

Puccini - 1918 - set in 13C Florence

Buoso Donati has died leaving all his riches to the monks. Rinuccio calls in Schicci to alter the will. This he does by pretending to be the dying Buoso and revising the will - but he cunningly leaves all the items of value to himself.

Starts with the greedy relatives of Donati gathered around his dead body hunting for the will...

[Short, and usually done with either "Sister Angelica" or "Il Tabarro" or sometimes both].

THE GIRL OF THE GOLDEN WEST

Puccini - 1910 - Californian gold-mining town - 1849

Schoolmistress/bar owner, Minnie, falls in love with a mysterious stranger, Johnson, who is later recognised as the robber-in-chief Ramerrez. Minnie invites him to supper but they are discovered and he is injured. Minnie gambles for his life and wins, but he is recaptured; and when he is condemned to be hung she rescues him yet again.

Starts in the evening in a bar where the bartender is lighting the candles and miners are entering - a stranger sits homesick...

THE GOLDEN COCKEREL

Rimsky Korsakov - 1910 - Fairy-tale

Old King Dodon is given a remarkable Golden Cockerel by his Astrologer. His army is defeated and he falls in love with the wicked Queen of Shemakha and is about to marry her. He is challenged by his Astrologer, who he strikes dead - but the Cockerel then kills him.

Starts with the King complaining to everyone that he used to conquer others, but now they conquer him...

GÖTTERDÄMMERUNG – [see "Twilight of the Gods" which is part 3 of the "Ring Cycle" and on pg 72].

HANSEL AND GRETEL

Humperdinck - 1893 – Fairyland

Two children Hansel and Gretel are sent into the woods to pick strawberries but are overtaken by nightfall. They wake to see a house made of sweetmeats which they start to eat. A witch opens the door and imprisons them.

The witch likes to roast children in her oven, but Gretel cunningly gets the witch to show her how to get into the oven and traps her in it - the witch is cooked and all her victims come alive again.

Starts in a cottage with Hansel making brooms and Gretel knitting...

HUGH THE DROVER

Vaughan Williams - 1924 - set in mediaeval England

Mary is to be married to John the Butcher, but he is a rich bully and she much prefers Hugh the Drover. The rivals box and Hugh wins - but gets locked up in the stocks as a suspected spy. Mary releases him and after various events he is shown to be innocent.

Starts with a bustling fair in the Cotswolds with showman and ballad seller...

THE HUGUENOTS

Meyerbeer - 1836 - set in France, 1572.

The Queen wants Raoul (Huguenot man) and Valentine (Catholic woman) to marry in order to unite Catholics and Protestants. But Raoul declines because of Valentine's earlier association with the Comte de Nevers (Catholic), whom she marries. Raoul overhears plotting by the Catholics to massacre the Huguenots, and finally the Comte de Nevers is killed. Raoul and Valentine always loved each other, and now they are brought together. But then they are shot.

Starts with the Comte de Nevers entertaining friends and awaiting a last guest (a Huguenot)...

IDOMENEO

Mozart - 1781 - set in Mythical Crete.

Cretan King Idomeneo escapes shipwreck on his return from the Trojan War by making a deal with Neptune (the sea-god) to sacrifice the first living creature he meets. This turns out to be his son Idamante, desired by Greek Elektra, but who happens to be in love with conquered Trojan prisoner Ilia, King Priam's daughter, who loves him in return. Idomeneo exiles his son to save him but Neptune objects, only relenting on condition that the King abdicates in favour of his son. So everyone rejoices except Elektra.

Starts with Ilia singing of her conquerors and her love for Idamante - and he comes on and sings of his for her...

L'INCORONAZIONE DI POPPEA
- [see "Coronation of Poppea" pg 30]

INTO THE WOODS

Sondheim - 1987 - Fairyland

A Baker and his Wife have many adventures involving various traditional characters: Cinderella, Little Red Riding Hood, Jack of the Beanstalk and Rapunzel.

In the *first* half the Witch sets four things for the couple to find in order to remove a spell of "barrenness" (Milky-white cow, blood-red cape, corn-yellow hair and gold slipper) and they have light-hearted adventures achieving them.

The *second* half works up to a climax of death and destruction all round (even the Narrator is not exempt) - finishing with the death of the Giant and a reprise with "morals" by all the characters.

Starts with the cottages of the characters in the woods and Cinderella sweeping the kitchen, Jack milking his cow and the Baker and his wife baking - whilst a Narrator tells the story...

[Sometimes classified as "Musical Theatre"].

IPHIGÉNIE EN AULIDE

Gluck - 1774 - Trojan War

Greek King Agamemnon has vowed to sacrifice his daughter Iphigenia to Diana in return for a favourable wind to take his fleet to Troy. Iphigenia is lured to Aulis on the pretext of marrying Achilles, but they fall in love.

Achilles prevents the sacrifice, and the High Priest reinterprets the oracle to announce that the gods are appeased and will grant the fair weather wanted by Agamemnon.

Starts with King Agamemnon feeling remorseful and torn between duty and love...

IPHIGÉNIE EN TAURIDE

Gluck - 1779 - after Trojan War

Iphigenia is a Priestess at the temple of Diana, and King Thoas needs a sacrifice to ward off danger. Orestes is a possible victim, being full of remorse for a crime he says he has committed (killing his mother Clytemnestra) and a bit mad; and he is about to be sacrificed by Iphigenia when she recognises him as her brother. There is general confusion involving also Orestes' friend Pylade, and the King is killed - but goddess Diana pardons all.

Starts in the Temple of Diana where Iphigenia is talking of a misfortune back at home...

ITALIAN GIRL IN ALGIERS (Italiana in Algeri)

Rossini - 1808 - set in palace of the Bey of Algiers

The Bey (Ruler) is feeling bored with his wife Elvira when he hears of Isabella wrecked on his shores - and adds her to his harem immediately. She was travelling with an aged comic admirer (Taddeo) and was searching for her lost lover Lindoro, who is now a slave in service with the Bey.

The two lovers team up and play tricks on the Bey, most importantly fooling him into signing up as a "Pappatacci" (ie complacent husband) which he does with style, not realising that the lovers are about to escape by boat - which he takes rather well, deciding to love his wife after all and forgive everyone.

Starts with a chorus of eunuchs in the harem (surprisingly including basses) lamenting the lot of women, whilst the Bey's wife Elvira bemoans her husband's lack of interest...

JENUFA

Janacek - 1904 - set beside a mill in the mountains

This is a two-man love triangle in which the girl Jenufa has had a baby by her first lover (Steva), a drunkard who has now abandoned her in favour of other girls. Jenufa's stepmother is appalled at the scandal and her first solution is to tell Steva to marry the girl - but he refuses, being now engaged to the Mayor's daughter - so the stepmother decides to drown the baby.

Steva's half-brother Laca has loved Jenufa from the start and she accepts his advances... but when the dead baby is unexpectedly discovered the stepmother's crime is exposed - but Jenufa and Laca are now firmly in love.

Starts outside the mill with the old grandmother, Laca and Jenufa - who is thinking of her lover Steva who has abandoned her to enlist in the army...

JULIUS CAESAR

Handel - 1724 - set in Egypt, 48 AD

Caesar has just defeated the Egyptians, and queen Cleopatra fancies him, whilst king Ptolemy fancies the dead Roman general Pompey's widow, Cornelia.

Cleopatra frustrates an attempt on Caesar's life, but Cornelia refuses Ptolemy - who dies in a duel. Caesar and Cleopatra are united in the end.

Starts with an Egyptian chorus greeting the victorious Romans - and Julius Caesar enters...

KATYA KABANOVA

Janacek - 1921 - set in small town on the Volga 1860

Set in a period when the strict Slavonic matriarchy was being ousted by a more emancipated generation, young Boris and Katya find themselves deeply in love, though Katya is already married (unhappily to a drunkard) and each is still under the thumb of the older generation.

A less inhibited couple (Barbara and Vanya) demonstrate how free love can operate, and contrive to get the pair to meet on an idyllic summer night. But when Katya's husband (Tikhon) appears, she is impelled to confess her passion for Boris, and there is drama on all sides followed by quiet reconciliation - and a quiet suicide by Katya.

Starts on the banks of the Volga outside the Kabanov house with Vanya and others talking about the oppressive parents... and then Boris's problems are slowly explained to us...

KING PRIAM

Tippett - 1962 - set in Troy in antiquity

A diffuse story based on "decision" situations, heroic love and suffering, starting with Trojan King Priam's decision to have his son Paris killed because of a prophecy; but the child survives, only to elope with Greek Queen Helen - sparking a Greek/Trojan war.

Greek hero Achilles (after having his lover killed by Priam's first son Hector) appears dramatically and kills Hector. Hector's brother Paris now feels he has to kill Achilles as retribution, so that when Priam begs Hector's body from Achilles they talk of vulnerability - not unreasonable as most of the men get killed before the end.

Starts with trumpets and discussion of Queen Hecuba's dream that her newly-born son Paris will cause King Priam's death.

LADY MACBETH OF MTSENSK

Shostakovich - 1934 - Soviet Russia

Bored with her inadequate husband Zinovy, Katerina makes passionate love with labourer Sergei. But she is spotted by her father-in-law, Boris, who beats up Sergei but is in turn poisoned by Katerina. When her husband Zinovy returns he is murdered by Katerina and Sergei, who then get married.

Unfortunately a drunken peasant finds Zinovy's body and tells the police, so that the couple finish up ruined and on the road to Siberia - arguing . And Sergei gets a new woman, who finishes up in the river with Katerina...

Starts with Katerina on her bed bemoaning her boring life as her disagreeable father-in-law nags her to produce an heir...

[About the hardships and triumphs of Russian women]

LOHENGRIN

Wagner - 1850 - set in 10C Germany

Elsa is incorrectly accused by her guardian Frederick of killing her brother Gottfried, but a mysterious Knight appears in a boat drawn by a swan. The Knight challenges and defeats Frederick and marries Elsa on condition she does not seek to know who he is.

Frederick's wife Ortrud now gets Elsa worried enough to ask the fatal question. The Knight is attacked by Frederick, whom he kills; then reveals himself as Lohengrin, son of King Parsifal (guardian of the Holy Grail). He will now have to depart - but not before transforming the swan back into long-lost Gottfried.

Starts on a river plain with Henry 1st and nobles listening to Count Frederick's strange tale...

THE LOVE FOR THREE ORANGES

Prokofiev - 1921 - set in "playing card" kingdom.

The son and heir (and hypochondriac) Prince of the King of Clubs cannot be cured and wicked Clarissa will succeed to the throne unless the Prince is made to laugh. Comedians and spectacles are arranged, but the only thing that makes him laugh is witch Fata Morgana falling over, which irritates her so much as to curse him to "fall in love with three oranges".

He has many adventures with a Magician, fat Cook, devil Farfarello, castle and ribbon until the oranges produce beautiful girls, the last of which is saved for him (by the audience) but promptly turned into a rat and then back again into a Princess - amongst general climactic confusion.

Starts in the King's palace where doctors grouped around his prostrate son pronounce him incurable - unless he can be made to laugh...

LUCIA DI LAMMERMOOR

Donizetti - 1835 - set in 17C Scotland

Lucy loves Edgar, but her brother Sir Henry (who has wrongly grabbed the estate from him) gets her to recoup family fortunes by marrying rich Sir Arthur instead, using a forged letter to do this. Later Edgar challenges Sir Henry - but Lucy has gone mad and murdered her husband, and as she dies Edgar stabs himself in despair.

Starts in a grove near the castle with Henry learning from Norman that Lucy and Edgar are meeting...

LULU

Berg - 1937 - set in a German city at end of 19C

Lulu is a sexy woman who attracts and discards men, and is surrounded by strange characters in strange circumstances: a painter, a comic newspaper editor, his contemplative writer son, an infatuated schoolboy, a lesbian and a comic old man.

An interlude between scenes is occupied by a film of Lulu being condemned for murdering the writer, and her hospitalisation for cholera. More adventures in a brothel and in a London slum culminate with a final pick-up - Jack the Ripper, who murders her.

Starts with Lulu dressed as Pierrot being painted by the painter watched by the newspaper editor and (later) his son...

["Twelve-tone" music and a bit of finishing by others].

MACBETH

Verdi - 1847 - set in Scotland, 1040

Spurred on by the enigmatic prophecies of three witches and his over-ambitious wife, General Macbeth aspires to the crown of Scotland, and achieves this by murdering King Duncan (a guest at his castle) and fellow-General Banquo.

But then he is overcome with remorse, and gives himself away to the nobles by responding to "Banquo's ghost" at a banquet; and his wife goes mad - sleepwalking - and dies. His reign of terror is eventually brought to an end by a defeat in war.

Starts on a spooky heath where Macbeth consults the witches...

MADAM BUTTERFLY

Puccini - 1904 - set in Japan, 1904

Lieutenant Pinkerton marries a pretty Japanese girl (Butterfly) with no intention of remaining faithful. He returns to America and comes back three years later with an American wife to claim his son by Butterfly. Butterfly kills herself.

Starts with Pinkerton in his rented garden talking with his marriage broker..

THE MAGIC FLUTE

Mozart - 1791 - set in pantomime Egypt

Following rescue from a pantomime serpent and an encounter with a bird-catcher (Papageno), Egyptian prince Tamino is induced to desire Queen of the Night's daughter Pamina, currently held prisoner by Priest Sarastro - but available to him if rescued...

Given a Magic Flute (for Tamino) and a Chime of Bells (for Papageno), the two are guided by boys into weird adventures before Tamino meets Pamina - his true love.

Now follow theatrical excursions culminating in trials by fire and water before the lovers are finally qualified, blessed and hymned.

Starts with Tamino meeting a snake, which three Ladies of the Night kill..

[Imagery based on Masonic ritual and pantomime.]

THE MAKROPULOS AFFAIR

Janacek - 1926 - set in Prague, 1920

In 1565 Court Physician Makropulos found an elixir of life which was given to his daughter - who still lives, retaining the initials "E.M". In the 19th century she had an affair with a Baron Prus, and had a son who reappeared to claim the Baron's estate some time later. She now appears in 1920 as a Scottish singer Emilia Marty - a cold character bored with life and wanting to die...

The action is a complicated detective story introducing "E.M." in different centuries and gradually revealing the situation. Eventually she announces her need for another dose of elixir, without which she suddenly ages and dies, but not before handing the secret formula to someone else - who tosses it into the fire.

Starts in a lawyer's office where the claim on the estate is being discussed, and Emilia herself appears, keen to study the case - with amazing insight into the details....

MANON

Massenet - 1884 - set in 18C French court.

Des Grieux falls in love at first sight with attractive but wayward Manon, and she manages an elopement under the noses of two older men. However a rich nobleman (Bretigny) entices her away and grief-stricken Des Grieux becomes an abbé.

Manon is upset by this and returns to Des Grieux, but he starts gambling and gets arrested; and then Manon also gets arrested and condemned to deportation - and desperate, he tries to rescue her - but she dies.

Starts outside a crowded inn. Lescaut enters and talks of Manon...

MANON LESCAUT

Puccini - 1893 - set in 18C French court

Des Grieux falls in love at first sight with attractive but wayward Manon, and she manages an elopement under the noses of two older men. One of them (Geronte) entices her away with his riches, but she soon switches back her affections to Des Grieux, unfortunately hesitating too long to collect her beloved jewellery.

She is caught by Geronte and sentenced to deportation to America, to be followed by Des Grieux in whose arms she dies at the end.

Starts outside a crowded inn. A coach disgorges Manon, Lescaut and Geronte..

THE MARRIAGE OF FIGARO

Mozart - 1786 - set in 18C Spain

The Count's servants Figaro and Susanna are getting married, and his page Cherubino has an infatuation for all women. The Count rather fancies Susanna, and the situation enrages him to such an extent that he orders Cherubino into the army and tries to bed Susanna himself.

His ever-faithful wife, the Countess, disguises herself as Susanna and meets the Count on a love tryst in the garden at night - thus humiliating him so that all can be forgiven (but with the moral pointed).

Starts with Susanna at her mirror while Figaro paces out the room they have been offered...

MARY STUART

Donizetti - 1834 - Set in London and Fotheringay, 1567

Elizabeth, Queen of England (Protestant) has imprisoned her cousin Mary, Queen of Scots (Catholic, and with designs on the throne). Elizabeth's favourite, Earl Leicester, who she discovers has been attracted to Mary, persuades Elizabeth to pay Mary a visit.

In a dramatic confrontation Elizabeth accuses Mary of murdering her husband and Mary retorts by insulting her, and is thus condemned to death.

In *London* Elizabeth, torn with indecision, eventually signs the death warrant (asking Leicester to be present as a penance), and in *Fotheringay* Mary hears the confession of her servant Talbot which seems to clear her of the murder - but the execution proceeds nevertheless....

Starts with courtiers at Westminster awaiting the arrival of Elizabeth, who is rumoured to be about to marry the King of France...

A MASKED BALL

Verdi - 1859 - set in Stockholm, 1858 or Boston.

King Gustavus loves his friend's wife and discovers that she returns his love, but is attempting to suppress it. The friend (Anckarstroem) assumes his wife is unfaithful and joins a group plotting the King's death. Anckarstroem stabs him at a masked ball - but his wife is revealed to have been guiltless all the time.

Starts in the King's house where he is shown the guests and recognises Amelia - his love...

THE MASTERSINGERS

Wagner - 1868 - set in 16C Nuremberg.

Young Knight Walther is in love with Eva. Her father has promised her to the singer who wins the prize of Mastersinger at the coming festival. Walther attempts to join their Union but is rejected as his song doesn't fit their rules. Hans Sachs recognises Walther's talent and teaches him how to fit his melody to the rules whilst still keeping it new. The Clerk Beckmesser, who marked Walther so badly, is also hoping to win Eva and steals the song from Sachs' workshop believing it to be his, but makes a complete mess of singing it. At Sachs's behest Walther then sings his song the way it deserves, wins the prize, gains acceptance as a Mastersinger and wins Eva - to general rejoicing.

Starts in church with the congregation singing and Walther nodding at Eva...

THE MERRY WIVES OF WINDSOR

Nicolai - 1849 - set in Windsor, Henry IV time

Rotund jovial buffoon Sir John Falstaff has sent love letters to two married ladies who plot to trap him in a laundry basket and dump him in the Thames. Later on he is tormented by the ladies dressed up as fairies in a forest at night. He survives undamaged.

Starts in the garden between their houses as the ladies compare the love-letters he has sent them...

THE MIDSUMMER MARRIAGE

Tippett - 1955 - set in a mythical present.

This unique opera is an exploration of the mysteries of masculinity and femininity expressed by a pair of archetypal lovers, Mark, a warm and soft young man and Jenifer, a cold and hard young woman ("I want truth not love") coming to terms with their differences as they approach marriage. They also experience parental opposition and misunderstandings, and are contrasted with a pair of lovers (Jack and Bella) who sail through life totally unaware of these problems.

The opera makes use of staircases (up for *female truth* and down for *male assertion* - symbolised by Athena and Dionysus), ritual dances of pursuer and quarry, clairvoyance and the Ancients, carnal love and fertility, to take us nearer the magical and ritual forces of nature - culminating in truth and the triumph of young love.

Starts with a stage picture of a wooded hill top with temple, friends, dancers etc and eventually Jenifer repulsing the advances of Mark...

[Obscure action but intoxicating music]

A MIDSUMMER NIGHT'S DREAM

Britten - 1960 - Fairyland/Classical Times/England

Fairy King Oberon is at odds with his Queen Tytania over a changeling boy she will not give up to him. He sends the spirit Puck to find a love potion which will make her fall for the first living thing she sees on awakening.

Meanwhile two pairs of lovers are escaping arranged marriages and travelling through the forest, quarrelling en route. Oberon tells Puck to use the potion on one of the men but he gets it disastrously wrong.

Tradesmen, preparing an entertainment for the Court are rehearsing in the forest. The weaver, Bottom, has an ass's head put on his shoulders by Puck, and when Tytania wakes she falls in love with him. Eventually the antidote is given to those needing it, and all ends happily.

Starts with fairies in a spooky wood...

MIKADO (Or the Town of Titipu)

Sullivan - 1885 - set in Japan

The Mikado's son, Nanki-Poo, fleeing in troubadour disguise from a threatened marriage with aged Katisha, is seeking his beloved Yum-Yum when he finds that her guardian, Ko-Ko (High Executioner) wants to marry her himself.

A happy arrangement is made with Ko-Ko that Nanki-Poo can marry Yum-Yum for only one month after which he will be decapitated. But then Ko-Ko discovers a law stating that an executed man's wife has to be buried alive – not good news for Yum-Yum.

The Mikado mistakenly thinks that Ko-Ko has already killed his heir, Nanki-Poo, which means that Ko-Ko has to be boiled in oil. His only escape would be to marry aged Katisha. He agrees, and Yum-Yum and Nanki-Poo reappear alive and married, and all are happy.

Starts with strolling Gentlemen of Japan broken into by Nanki-Poo in minstrel disguise seeking Yum-Yum...

["Savoy Opera". Libretto by Gilbert].

NABUCCO (Nebuchadnezzar)

Verdi - 1842 - set in Jerusalem and Babylon - 586 BC

Of the supposed daughters (Fenena and Abigaille) of Babylonian King Nabucco only Fenena is legitimate, but they are rivals for the Regency over the defeated Jews.

In the battle Fenena becomes a hostage of the Jews. She and her Jewish jailor Ismaele fall in love, and she later converts to Judaism; but Ismaele is also desired by Abigaille.

In a complicated plot where Nabucco goes insane, Abigaille grabs the Regency but gets two come-uppances before Nabucco is converted and the Jews are freed.

Starts with the Jews lamenting their defeat by Babylonians and praying for the Temple to be saved...

[Opera taken as symbol of freedom following oppression].

NORMA

Bellini - 1831 - set in Gaul 50BC

Priestess Norma has broken her vow of chastity and borne two sons to Pollione, Roman pro-Consul, but he has now fallen in love with Adalgisa, a temple virgin, and persuaded her to elope with him.

Despairing, Norma decides against killing her sons and instead sends them to Adalgisa asking her to be a mother to them.

But Adalgisa will not hear of this sacrifice and renounces Pollione, who then attempts to abduct her from the temple, is discovered and condemned to death for sacrilege. Norma confesses and enters the funeral pyre in his stead, only to be followed by Pollione, whose love has been rekindled by her heroism.

Starts with the Druids in a sacred grove. The high priest is begging the gods to rouse the people to war against the Romans..

ORFEO

Monteverdi - 1607 - Greek myths

Orfeo and Eurydice are happily married, but the gods are envious and kill Eurydice.

Orfeo sings his way into hell and persuades underworld Pluto to let Eurydice come back to life.

Pluto agrees she can follow him back *provided he does not look to see if she is following him* - a condition which he fails to keep, thus losing her.

After a prologue Shepherds and Nymphs rejoice at the wedding of Orpheo and Euridice...

ORPHEUS AND EURIDICE

Gluck - 1762 - Greek gods

Orpheus visits the tomb of his beloved Euridice and is given permission by god Zeus to use his music to try to persuade the underworld god Pluto to release her back to life.

But the condition is that he must lead her out of hell *without looking back*. He fails to do this and Euridice immediately dies - but the god of love (Amor) takes pity on them and saves her.

Starts in a grotto beside the tomb of Euridice where Orpheus and his friends are mourning...

OTHELLO

Verdi - 1887 - set in 15C Cyprus

Othello, a Moorish Admiral, and Desdemona are blissfully happy together, but evil Iago ignites and then fans Othello's jealousy so efficiently that Othello eventually kills his wife in a fury and then kills himself.

Iago does this by discrediting Othello's captain Cassio, getting him sacked and then set up as Desdemona's lover. He plants a handkerchief which was given to her by Othello on Cassio to "prove" her infidelity.

Starts in a stormy harbour in Cyprus. Othello's ship arrives and he disembarks...

I PAGLIACCI

Leoncavallo - 1892 - set in Calabria 1865

The wife (Nedda) of a travelling clown (Canio) is unfaithful. When he finds out he is so upset as to interrupt his performance as Pulchinello to stab her and her lover (Silvio).

Starts with a head through the curtain and then a crowded Feast of the Assumption with the Players on parade...

[Short opera usually played with "Cavalleria Rusticana", which, together, are known colloquially as "Cav and Pag"].

PARSIFAL

Wagner - 1882 - set in Spain

Amfortas, the warden of the Kingdom of the Holy Grail, lies at Monsalvat injured by a sacred spear and can only be cured by a guileless innocent. Parsifal appears as a youth and later resists the seductress Kundry's advances, thus destroying the Magician Klingsor and thereby acquiring the spear. After many years he returns to Monsalvat, cures Amfortas and joins the Knights of the Holy Grail.

Starts with old Gurnemanz and two young esquires who are woken up and start to pray...

PELLÉAS AND MÉLISANDE

Debussy - 1902 - set in France

King's grandson Golaud finds and marries Melisande, but while talking to his brother Pelleas she accidentally drops Golaud's ring into a well. It had magic powers and its loss injures Golaud, so he sends the pair back to find it.

But they fall in love and Golaud becomes jealous. He proclaims his wife's infidelity and attacks her, but Pelleas and Melisande declare their love to be true, so Golaud kills Pelleas - but, remorseful, he then has to watch Melisande as she dies.

Starts in a forest where Golaud is lost. He finds Melisande beside a well...

PETER GRIMES

Britten - 1945 - set in Suffolk, late 18C

Peter Grimes is a solitary and visionary fisherman who is accused of abusing his boy apprentices. One dies at sea, the second falls over a cliff, but Peter is only dreaming of making a record catch and marrying his love the schoolteacher Ellen. When the latest apprentice dies the villagers round on Peter, and the demented man is advised to go out to sea and sink himself in his boat.

Starts in the moot hall with an inquest on Peter's first apprentice. The crowd of villagers are restless...

PORGY AND BESS

Gershwin - 1935 - set in negro Charleston, USA.

Drunk stevedore Crown kills a neighbour after losing at dice, and flees town leaving his girl Bess to be sheltered by cripple Porgy. They make a good couple, but Bess still hankers for Crown, going to a picnic where he appears and seduces her. A storm and various drownings precede Porgy stabbing Crown - and getting away with it. But Bess leaves him for drug pedlar "Sporting Life" in New York, and Porgy goes after her...

Starts outside tenements with singing and dancing. Clara is singing a lullaby to her baby...

PRINCE IGOR

Borodin - 1890 - set in Russia, 1185

Prince Igor and his son Vladimir go to battle against the Khan. They are defeated and imprisoned, but the Khan's daughter Kontchaknova falls in love with Vladimir. After a feast Igor yearns for his wife and escapes, but his son hesitates and is welcomed to marry the girl. Igor is welcomed home by his wife.

Starts in Golitzky's house where he shows he is important..

.

THE QUEEN OF SPADES

Tchaikovsky - 1890 - set in St Petersburg

Eligible Prince Yeletsky is betrothed to Lisa, but she falls in love with poor Herman. Her grand-mother, the Countess, has a secret enabling her to win at cards, and Herman tries to get it. He accidentally kills the Countess in the process - but Lisa forgives him.

Herman thinks he will never learn the secret, but his victim's ghost appears and tells him. When he next meets Lisa he spurns her. She jumps off a bridge. He gambles his all, loses and stabs himself.

Starts in gardens in St Petersburg where children are playing and nannies talking. Herman enters with friend...

THE RAKE'S PROGRESS

Stravinsky - 1951 - set in 18C England

Anne and Tom are happily betrothed, but Tom is taken over by a stranger Nick Shadow (the devil) who instigates various disastrous adventures: (a) going to London to collect an inheritance, (b) visiting a brothel, (c) marrying a bearded lady Baba the Turk, (d) investing in a magic bread machine.

Anne tries to rescue him but he eventually goes bankrupt. Nick eventually makes it clear that he wants Tom's soul, but a game of cards can decide it. When Tom wins he goes mad, dying in Anne's arms thinking he is Adonis and she Venus.

Starts with Anne and Tom rejoicing in the summer whilst her father Trulove mutters doubts about him...

RHINEGOLD [First part or Prelude to Ring]

Wagner - 1876 - set in legendary Rhineland

The dwarf Alberich renounces love in order to acquire the gold in the Rhine, making a magic Ring and helmet from it. Chief god Wotan tricks him out of both Ring and gold in order to pay the giants Fasolt and Fafner for building his wonderful new castle (Valhalla). Aggrieved Alberich lays a curse on the ring so that one of the giants kills the other and transforms himself into a dragon to guard the treasure.

Starts with Alberich viewing Rhine Maidens swimming..

RIGOLETTO *Verdi - 1851 - set in 17C Italy*

The libertine Duke of Mantua seduces Count Monterone's daughter and then assumes student disguise to seduce Gilda, the daughter of hunchback jester Rigoletto. Rigoletto finds out and plots to have the Duke killed (by Sparafucile) using the assassin's sister as decoy. Gilda decides to save her lover's life by dying in his stead, so when Rigoletto unties the sack containing the body he finds it is his daughter.

Starts with a ball in the Duke's palace. An angry Count Monterone rushes in...

THE RING [also called the "Ring Cycle" or "Ring of the Nibelung]. *To be pedantic, it consists of a Prologue and three parts – making four operas.*

This sequence of *Rheingold, Valkyrie, Siegfried and Twilight of the Gods* is unlike any other opera, a parable of human existence of cosmic dimensions which is treated as a semi-religion by many devotees. Perhaps it's about morals, good and evil, or even sex.

Viewed another way we have Nordic gods squabbling and devising their own downfall. And on another, more fairy-tale, plane we see dwarves, a Magic gold ring, treasure, castles in the sky, gods and mortals, knights and war-maidens, heroes and gods in human form, magic swords, walls of flames, mountains and dramatic lighting effects - and of course powerful drama and long-drawn-out richly scored dreamy music...

IL RITORNO D'ULISSE IN PATRIA

Monteverdi - 1641 - Greek Mythology

Ulysses has adventures making his way home to his wife Queen Penelope. Disguised as an old man he reveals himself to his son Telemacus and then finds his wife is surrounded by suitors. In a contest he kills them all, and after revealing his identity is reunited with his wife.

Starts in the palace with Penelope bemoaning her loneliness with Ulysses away...

RODELINDA *Handel - 1725 – set in heroic Italy*

Grimoaldo has deposed King Bertarido (who has pretended death and gone into hiding) and fancies his queen (Rodelinda). He eventually relents and returns husband to wife. During the action the king sees his tomb, meets his wife, goes to prison, escapes, has a pastoral reverie etc..

Starts in Rodelinda's apartments where she bemoans the death of her husband - but he's actually alive..

DER ROSENKAVALIER

Richard Strauss - 1911 - set in 19C Germany

The Marschallin knows her young lover Octavian will soon turn to someone of his own age, and she asks him to do a favour for her kinsman Baron Ochs (a repulsive boor) by taking a rose to young Sophie as a symbol of his intent to marry her. However Sophie and Octavian fall in love, and Octavian decides to expose the Baron.

Octavian dresses up as a girl (Mariandel) and arranges an assignation for the Baron at an inn, where ghosts and phoney relatives are introduced to discredit him - and with the aid of the Marschallin the lovers are united.

Starts in the Marschallin's bedroom where young Octavian is embracing the Marschallin...

RUSALKA

Dvorak - 1901 - Fairyland

Rusalka, the daughter of the Spirit of the Lake wants to become human so that she can marry the Prince, and the Witch organises this but warns her that she will become unable to speak, and if her lover is unfaithful both will be damned for ever.

The Prince is puzzled by her speechlessness at their wedding and dances with a Princess instead. When Rusalka intervenes he abandons her and she is transformed into a will o' the wisp.

Later the lonely Prince wanders by the Lake and encounters Rusalka again, but she warns him that her kiss will kill him - and he dies in her arms.

Starts on the lake shore with Wood nymphs tempting the good-natured Spirit of the Lake out of his abode, to be followed by his daughter Rusalka telling of her love...

SALOME

Richard Strauss - 1905 - New Testament

Sexy young Salome finds her ogling stepfather Herod and his rich friends distasteful, and uses her wiles over the guard to produce the imprisoned Jokanaan (John the Baptist); and when he arrives she tries to kiss him (and the guard kills himself).

Herod nags her to dance in front of him, and reluctantly she agrees in return for his promise to grant her her "wish". She dances and then asks for "Jokanaan's head" on a platter. This she kisses - which disgusts Herod so much that he orders her to be killed too.

Starts on Herod's terrace at night. The Captain of the Guard sings of Salome's beauty...

SAMSON AND DALILA

Saint-Saens - 1877 - Old Testament

Samson revives the fortunes of the suppressed Israelites by killing the Philistine bully Abimelech. However the Philistine High Priest gets Dalila to seduce Samson, and he is blinded.

At a large gathering of the Philistines Samson manages to grab the pillars of the temple and pull them down on top of the multitude.

Starts in the town square where the conquered multitude bemoan their fate - until Samson arrives...

SEMELE

Handel - 1744 - Roman gods

King's daughter Semele and god Jupiter are enamoured.

Jupiter's wife Juno plots vengeance. First she gets the god of sleep (Somnus) to give Jupiter such erotic dreams that he cannot refuse Semele's demands. Then Juno disguises herself as Semele's sister and tempts Semele to ask Jupiter to show himself as a god – which will mean she must die.

Semele makes Jupiter swear to grant her a request, and when he agrees asks him to appear before her as a god. He cannot persuade her otherwise - but from her ashes arises a phoenix.

Starts with ceremonies in Thebes; Juno accepts a sacrifice and crowd rejoices...

SEMIRAMIDE

Rossini - 1823 - set in ancient Babylon.

Queen Semiramide murders the King assisted by Prince Assur - who hopes to get the crown; but actually Semiramide loves another (Arsace).

A prophecy gives Arsace the succession, and this so enrages Assur that he attempts to kill Arsace. He is foiled by Semiramide who has learned that Arsace is her son and she takes the fatal wound herself. He is proclaimed King and avenger of his father's murder.

IL SERAGLIO

Mozart - 1782 - set in mediaeval Turkey.

Constanze and her maid have been captured by pirates and put in a Turkish harem, and her betrothed (Belmonte, a young nobleman) has come to rescue her. The plan is for his servant to get a menial job in the harem and introduce Belmonte as an architect, and then get the guard (Osmin, a comic fool) drunk.

It all misfires and they are imprisoned, but the Pasha is compassionate and lets everyone go so that Constanze and Belmonte (and the servant and the maid) can be happily united.

Starts with Belmonte outside the Pasha's house spying Osmin singing a love song...

LA SERVA PADRONA

Pergolesi - 1752 - set in 18C Italy

Uberto asks his servant Vespone to find him a wife. His maid Serpina suggests herself as candidate, but has to employ a ruse to achieve her ambition. She gets Vespone to dress up as her most distasteful fiancé, and this inspires Uberto to rescue her by marrying her himself.

Starts with Uberto dressing to go out but waiting ages for chocolate...

[A small scale opera - 3 actors and string quartet]

SIEGFRIED [Part 3 of Ring cycle].

Wagner - 1876 - Legendary forests etc..

Sieglinde and Siegmund's son Siegfried has been brought up by dwarf Mime, and is obviously a hero as he successfully reforges his father's magic sword and determines to get the Ring from the Dragon.

The Ring (and helmet) is exactly what Mime wants, but so too does his brother Alberich, who warns the Dragon. This is of little avail as Siegfried has no trouble killing it - and a bird helps him realise Mime would poison him for the Ring: so he kills Mime.

Prompted by the bird again Siegfried sets off to free a maiden asleep on a rock guarded by a ring of fire. The god Wotan (disguised as a Wanderer) bars his way - but Siegfried defeats him to reach and awaken Valkyrie Brunnhilde and find passionate love.

Starts in a cave with Mime trying to forge a sword...

SIMON BOCCANEGRA

Verdi - 1857 - set in 14C Italy

Goldsmith Paolo helps seafaring Simon Boccanegra to become Doge of Venice. Boccanegra hopes that this will enable him to marry nobly-born Maria, who has borne him a daughter. But as he is elected he hears that Maria has died and their daughter has vanished.

Now, twenty-five years later, Boccanegra discovers a foundling (Amelia) to be his long-lost daughter. She is in love with a young man called Adorno but is also desired by Boccanegra's old friend Paolo. When Boccanegra denies Amelia to him Paolo poisons him in revenge. Boccanegra dies blessing the young lovers. and hailing Adorno as the next Doge.

Starts with a prologue in the town square where Paolo tells Boccanegra that the citizens are ready to elect him Doge...

SISTER ANGELICA

Puccini - 1918 - set in a convent

Sister Angelica took the veil in expiation of the sin of giving birth to an illegitimate child, and is now visited by the Princess, her aunt, who requires her signature on a document.

The Sister asks after her child only to be told coldly that it died two years ago, and in despair takes poison, praying that she may not die in mortal sin. As she dies she sees a vision of the Virgin leading a little child towards her...

Starts with singing in a convent. Postulants enter followed by Sister Angelica...

[A Short opera]

THE SNOW MAIDEN

Rimsky-Korsakov - 1882 - Fairytale

Spring and winter were once in love and the Snow Maiden is their child. She has to live in the cold, for she would die if the sun-god glimpsed her. She is left in the care of the Spirit of the Wood as her parents go North, and attends a carnival where she falls for Lehl, who abandons her for another, whilst someone else (Miskir) falls in love with her - but she rejects him.

She wants to "love and be loved" so appeals to her mother, and her wish is granted. She and Miskir are about to be married when she is killed by the warmth of the sun - so Miskir throws himself into the lake.

Starts in the snow with the Snow Maiden blaming the birds for King Frost treating her as a slave.

LA SONNAMBULA

Bellini - 1831 - set in Swiss village - early 19C

Mill-owner's foster-daughter Amina is betrothed to a landowner Elvino, but suffers from sleepwalking. Unwittingly she enters the bedroom of the Lord of the Castle (who behaves honourably by leaving the room) and is later discovered in his bed by her betrothed, Elvino.

Elvino cannot understand the phenomenon of sleepwalking and so breaks off the engagement. He is about to marry another when Amina is seen walking in her sleep across a perilous mill bridge. It breaks dramatically ... but she survives, and she and Elvino are reconciled.

Starts on the village green where villagers are celebrating the forthcoming marriage of Amina and Elvino...

SWEENEY TODD

(The Demon Barber of Fleet Street).

Sondheim – 1979 – 19C London

Ex-barber Todd returns from exile with a grievance against corrupt Judge Turpin who fixed him up in order to rape his wife, now believed dead. Todd revisits his old home, now a pie shop run by a Mrs Lovett, who recognises him and lets him set up as a barber again. He gains clients by winning a contest against an Italian fraudster, Pirelli. However Pirelli learns of his past history and tries to blackmail him, and has to be murdered.

Coming in for a shave, Judge Turpin reveals his designs on Todd's daughter (now his ward), which precipitates Todd's resolve to kill him and as many clients as possible. Mrs Lovett will use the bodies to make better pies, and a routine with a special tilting barber's chair and chute down to an oven is established.

Todd gets his friend Anthony to trick his daughter Johanna out of Judge Turpin's asylum, after which the plot goes mad. Todd is eventually murdered himself, like most of the cast - but only after discovering that he has murdered his previous wife - seen throughout as a beggar woman.

Starts with Todd (and sailor-friend Anthony) returning from exile abroad - destitute but still carrying his precious razors…

IL TABARRO (Cloak)

Puccini - 1918 - set on a Parisian barge

Giorgetta has got tired of her elderly husband Michele and is irresistibly drawn to a young man - Luigi. They make an assignation, but Michele guesses what is going on and stabs Luigi. Michele covers him up with his cloak, and when Giorgetta arrives he reveals the corpse.

Starts with barge master Michele on his boat, and his wife offering wine to stevedores... [Short opera].

TANNHÄUSER

Wagner - 1845 - set in 13C Thuringia

Tannhauser has tasted immoral love with Venus but feels he must return to the world, so he decides to reform. But he is persuaded by the Landgrave and his followers to return to Court by being told (by friend Wolfram) that his earlier love, Elisabeth, has been pining for him - but as he is still partially under the spell of Venus he cannot resist singing praises to her, and is cast out. As he joins some pilgrims to Rome Elisabeth prays for their love.

He is rejected by the Pope and returns - though he still rejects the lure of Venus by calling Elisabeth's name; and as he sees her funeral procession approaching he falls across her corpse dying - and is finally redeemed.

Starts in front of castle of love - Tannhauser sings of Venus...

TOSCA *Puccini - 1900 - set in Rome*

Painter Cavaradossi hides a fugitive (Angelotti) from justice but the Chief of Police (Scarpia) finds the hiding place by torturing him and questioning his lover, Tosca. However Cavaradossi has broken the law and must die, so Tosca makes a deal with Scarpia to offer herself to him in return for a fake execution at which Cavaradossi must pretend to die - but will actually escape. Having got Cavaradossi's safe conduct she stabs Scarpia, but contrary to his agreement Scarpia has ordered live bullets and Cavaradossi is killed. About to be arrested, Tosca leaps to her death.

Starts in church. Escaped prisoner Angelotti finds keys and hides in a chapel..

LA TRAVIATA [Courtesan] *Verdi - 1857 - Paris, 1850*

Alfredo falls in love with Violetta, a courtesan dying of consumption, and persuades her to live with him. However his father Germont doesn't want such a scandalous person to be associated with his daughter, who is about to get married, so he asks Violetta to abandon Alfredo.

Later the heartbroken Alfredo meets her at a party and there is an unpleasant incident with her protector Baron Douphol. Then Alfredo finds out that she still loves him and was protecting him, and as he returns to make it up she dies.

Starts in Violetta's house. She is talking to a Dr Grenvil...

TRISTAN AND ISOLDE

Wagner - 1865 - Arthurian England

Tristan is bringing Isolde in his boat to Cornwall where she is to marry King Mark. Tristan and Isolde are in love with each other but unaware of each other's feelings, so Isolde despairingly tries to poison them both - but as the poison turns out to be a love potion they actually fall in love.

Their tryst at night while Mark is away hunting is betrayed by knight Melot, who wounds Tristan mortally, but he escapes and Isolde follows to arrive just as he dies.

Starts on board ship where Isolde (and later Tristan) both say they feel unloved...

TROILUS AND CRESSIDA

Walton - 1954 - set in 12C BC Troy

This is the story of Trojan Prince Troilus's tragic affair with his High Priest's daughter Cressida at a time of conflict with the Greeks. Separated initially by a prisoner exchange and isolated because Troilus's love letters are intercepted, Cressida is persuaded to marry Greek Prince Diomede. In the final crisis Troilus is killed and Cressida kills herself.

Starts with starving temple worshippers being told to negotiate with the Greeks, until the Captain urges them to fight...

THE TROJANS

Berlioz - 1863 - set in legendary Troy and Carthage

The FIRST part, set in Troy, tells the story of the "Trojan Horse", a Greek "Gift" that the gullible Trojans accepted but which disgorged soldiers at night - leading to the sack of Troy and the expulsion of Trojan hero Aeneas.

In the SECOND, set in Carthage, Dido the Queen is bemoaning the lack of a husband when Aeneas appears - just in time to defend her from some threatening Numidians, but not before becoming her lover. However "destiny" calls him and his fleet away to higher things such as founding a new empire in Italy, so abandoned Dido kills herself in despair.

Starts with the townsfolk of Troy rejoicing that their Greek captors have at last gone back home (but we suspect that actually they are planning a comeback)...

[Very long. Various versions, sometimes excluding the first part altogether].

IL TROVATORE

Verdi - 1853 - set in 15C Italy

Lady-in-Waiting Leonora loves a troubadour, but a rival Count stabs him - so, thinking he is dead, she enters a convent. But he recovers and rescues her.

The Count now captures a gipsy girl, but the troubadour is her secret foster-child and goes to her rescue - but is caught. Leonora's attempts to save the troubadour end in death for both, but the Count now finds that the troubadour he has killed was his brother (swapped in infancy) in disguise.

Starts in the atrium of the palace where the Captain of the Guard is watching out for the troubadour...

TURANDOT

Puccini - 1926 - set in China

Beautiful Princess Turandot will only marry the man who solves three puzzles, and anyone who fails must die.

Calaf (a King's son) falls in love with her and solves the puzzles, but still needs to win her heart. He offers a puzzle in return - to find his name - and she tortures his father's slave girl to no avail (the girl kills herself for love of Calaf). When Calaf reveals his name to be "love" Turandot's heart finally melts.

Starts beside the walls of Peking with a Royal Decree being read out...

THE TWILIGHT OF THE GODS

[Part 4 and end of the Ring Cycle].

Wagner - 1876 - Legendary

Hero Siegfried and Heroine Brunnhilde are united - but not for long, as evil dwarf Alberich's son Hagen gives him a potion causing him to switch affections to Gutrune as well as to assist in capturing Brunnhilde for Gunther. Hagen now stabs Siegfried in the back.

The Ring concludes with Brunnhilde riding into his funeral pyre and Valhalla (gods' palace) collapsing as the Ring returns to the Rhine Maidens.

Starts with the Norns (female beings) winding the skein of life - till it breaks...

THE VALKYRIE
[Part 2 of Ring Cycle]
Wagner - 1870 – Legendary

Desperate fugitive Siegmund finds Sieglinde in a forest hut and they fall in love not realising until later that they are siblings. When Sieglinde's unwanted and evil husband Hunding finds them together he challenges Siegmund.

Now Siegmund happens to be Wotan's son, and Wotan would have backed him if it weren't for his bossy wife Fricka (goddess of unbreakable marriage vows) who makes him order Valkyrie Brunnhilde to allow Hunding to kill Siegmund.

Brunnhilde refuses, so Wotan breaks Siegmund's sword with his spear, and Hunding kills Siegmund. Furious at losing his son, Wotan then kills Hunding. Rebellious Brunnhilde rescues Sieglinde - reassuring her that Sieglinde carries hero Siegfried in her womb. In return Wotan downgrades Brunnhilde to a slumbering mortal to be won by whoever finds her - so she asks for a "ring of fire" to ensure that he will be a Hero.

Starts with exhausted Siegmund entering Hunding's forest hut - to be followed by Sieglinde...

WOZZECK

Berg - 1925 - Set in the world of the common man

Soldier Wozzeck supports his lover Marie and their child by cutting the Captain's hair and assisting the Doctor - but Marie is inclined to flirt with the Drum Major. This winds up Wozzeck (he fantasises of blood) so much that he kills her.

After a brief episode in the arms of neighbour Margret he returns to the scene of his crime and just walks into the lake and drowns.

Starts with Wozzeck shaving the Captain, who is quite garrulous...

[Similar to but not strictly "twelve-tone" music].

XERXES

Handel – 1738 – Persia

King Xerxes is betrothed to Amastre but actually prefers Romilda, a commoner that his brother Arsamene fancies..

To make matters worse Romilda's sister Atalanta also desires Arsamene – thus setting the scene for a complicated plot in which women dress as men, love letters are assumed to be addressed to whoever reads them, and suicide and swordplay are threatened.

In the end Xerxes repents and blesses his brother's marriage.

Starts with Xerxes enjoying the shade of a tree …

[This aria is "Handel's Largo "].

[The opera is often classed as oratorio and includes comic elements. Confusion can be caused by the large number of characters starting with an "A" (note Romilda's father is Ariodate) and which might be women, or men sung by the opposite sex.]

ZAUBERFLÖTE – [see "Magic Flute" pg 40].

SOME THOUGHTS ABOUT CERTAIN PRACTICAL ASPECTS OF OPERA-GOING

WHEN OPERA IS GOOD IT'S MAGNIFICENT - BUT THERE CAN BE PROBLEMS...

Opera is the more considered part of the vast continuum of theatrical invention that is supported by drama, music, ballet, poetry and art. It seems to do particularly well with big human situations.

Perhaps most of the quality of opera comes from its music, but the whole can be far greater than the sum of its parts.

Although many operas were conceived to be heard in relatively small theatres, these days audiences are usually large, remote from the action and limited in what they can see and hear.

Productions are sometimes reinterpreted for the small screen or even broadcast on radio, but whilst these versions are better in some ways they are poor substitutes for the real thing.

The conflicting requirements of story, music and a large audience produce serious practical problems which are discussed below.

WHAT'S IT ALL ABOUT?

Early operas had a story that everyone knew, but nowadays most have a unique theatrical story-line that is defined, developed and concluded - but in reality usually only part is understood by an audience today.

I CAN'T UNDERSTAND THE WORDS

If the audience is expected to follow the action *as it develops* then major problems arise with hearing the words, especially if they are sung and there is over-emphasis on beauty of sound, a foreign language, insensitive music, too much reverberation or reliance on ladies' voices (usually less easy to understand).

THE MUSIC IS THE BEST PART

A passion for music is what drives most of us to opera in the first place, and what we experience must depend to some extent on our understanding as a listener or player - but in the end it's a gut reaction.

What our ears pick up is a fairly distant sound unlike that developed for radio, TV and CD which never relies on a microphone at the far end of the auditorium. Audiences can get slightly nearer to BBC quality by using good hearing aids - which can enhance slightly subnormal as well as normal hearing, but the ear adjusts, and few opera addicts are unhappy with our better opera houses.

HEARING PROBLEMS

Most men lose high frequency hearing early on in life, and cannot hear the important sibilants - but they may not be aware of it. This compromises their ability to understand speech because they are clogging up their mental capacity sorting out indistinct words.

EVERYONE THINKS DIFFERENTLY

We all "wire up" our brains in different ways in early infancy, something that educationalists cope with by presenting information in a variety of ways.

I CAN'T REMEMBER NAMES

In particular some people have problems with "Names" and "Plots", sometimes explained in terms of left and right lobe skills, and any solution needs to take these differences into account.

IT'S BEST TO READ A SYNOPSIS BEFOREHAND

The accepted solution has always been to read up the plot in advance, and whilst most regular opera-goers get by with reading a short programme synopsis there is great advantage in reading a full libretto. The fuller synopses in Kobbé come with relevant comments and musical illustrations, all of which can help - if your brain can take it in. It's worth trying different authors.

OPERA MANAGEMENT COULD HELP MORE

Other solutions involve the opera production side. Using smaller theatres whilst giving more performances seems to be a largely untried option these days, but it does return us to the sort of intimacy Mozart and Haydn assumed.

In the vast modern amphitheatre a narrator is easier to hear than a singer, and microphones can be used discreetly, whilst actors can be encouraged to enunciate clearly and position themselves to acoustical advantage.

There are the once controversial "surtitles" and other devices yet to be accepted - like a headphone commentary or back-of-seat displays - which could provide valuable incidental help, particularly in confirming where we are in the plot or even when the performance will end!

I REMEMBER SCENERY AND COSTUMES WERE STUNNING JUST AFTER THE WAR

Given progress on the understanding and hearing aspects, which should guarantee delights for the educated ear, there remains a current lack of delight for the educated eye. Good sets can add immeasurably to the atmosphere and meaning of an opera, but seem so often to be constrained by literary (and not visual) concepts. Many assume erroneously that this is an inevitable consequence of financial constraints. I think it is more a result of neglecting the visual arts at school. There is no excuse for sets being boring - we do have some inspired designers.

A QUIET WORD TO SYNOPSIS WRITERS

While we are considering practicalities I have struggled through more synopses than most and would mention common difficulties. Summaries need to be devised so that the characters developed in the minds of readers are readily identifiable on stage, and also so that it is easy to know where you are in the plot. A few "times" (as in the old BBC "timed" synopsis) can help, but an alternative is to mention key "moments" such as a chariot arriving or dramatic death.

CLARITY MATTERS MORE THAN STYLE

The style needs to be clear and absolutely unambiguous, even to the extent of adopting a crude "newspaper headline" style. It may be crude, but tying description to name (eg "evil dwarf Alberich") helps, and above all only one name should be used for each character.

Usually "Names" are less essential on stage than in plot summaries, and should be avoided if possible.

CLEAR TYPE ON WHITE PAPER

A good synopsis needs to be printed in large type, black on white - and absolutely not printed over fancy colour or graphics.

AUDIENCE GOOD MANNERS

A major problem is interrupted concentration and enjoyment due to other members of the audience.

Here are a few conventions that reduce irritation:-

> *Arrive on time, and a trace early if in the middle of a row of seats.*
>
> *Do not whisper or fidget during the overture.*
>
> *Do not clap except where convention allows - at moments which need to be learnt by experience.*
>
> *Coughs are very disruptive and can always be avoided. If prone to coughing have cough sweets lined up unwrapped ready for silent insertion into the mouth. In extremis stifle with a handkerchief, and choose a loud moment in the opera.*
>
> *Sneezes are equally disruptive. If a sneeze seems imminent press hard on the upper lip. This reduces blood supply to the nose and eases the irritation that triggers the sneeze.*
>
> *Quiet snoozing or gentle snoring is preferable to disruptive grunts, but a cup of coffee or bar of plain chocolate can restore concentration fairly quickly. Other disasters such as a seat collapsing or being rained on should be treated silently, causing as little disturbance as possible until the interval.*

ALIENATION KEEPS AUDIENCES AWAY

Getting all this right is a serious matter these days - as opera companies fight for their very existence. So it is sad that the professionals and opera buffs seem to be unaware of the alienation that some members of the audience feel if they fail to grasp a plot from the start.

It leads to frustration and anger and an anxiety to escape, especially if everyone else appears to be enjoying it. "Relax, sit back and savour the music" is what everyone advises, but that is not an option in this state of mind.

It's the main reason I stopped regular opera-going. But I know how wonderful opera can be if everything works, so I occasionally pay a visit - but now only if well prepared.

I hope these brief plot summaries will help you.

FEELING YOU WON'T BE ABLE TO FOLLOW THE PLOT IS VERY OFF-PUTTING.

It's not just a few people who have problems. Clarifying the daunting obscurity of plots is a key to unlocking enjoyment for the vast slice of the population who are anti-opera.

ELITISM

The preconception that only privileged people frequent opera is a mistaken cliché; the buffs are just as likely to be penurious, but they have found a way to cope with plots and inaudibility of words - as well as the cheaper seats where you can see and hear...

MANAGEMENT CAN HELP TOO – LARGER SEATS AND MORE LOOS!

Management can help by making the theatre well lit so that you can read your programme if you want to! At one time lights used to be kept on all the time for reading librettos.

The size and arrangement of seats and toilets in all opera venues (even new ones and particularly for ladies) needs attention. Audiences are getting "broader" in several senses of the word!

HELP PLEASE

The paradox of this book is that I have been motivated to write it because I find most plots so hard to grasp, but the people best placed to do this are those who find plots easy.

For that reason I would welcome constructive comments, improvements and additions - please write to the publisher, whose address can be obtained via your local bookshop.

ACKNOWLEDGMENTS

I am indebted to Don Moore, my wife Frances and various anonymous contributors for helpful comments and occasional total revisions.

COMPOSERS AND THEIR OPERAS – WITH DATES

By Composer in order of birthday grouped with their Operas as selected for this book in order of first performance.

MONTEVERDI 1567-1643
1607 Orfeo
1641 Ritorno D'Ulisse In Patria
1642 Coronation of Poppea

CAVALLI 1602-1676
1651 Calisto

PURCELL 1659-1695
1689 Dido and Aeneas

GAY 1685-1732
1728 Beggar's Opera

HANDEL 1685-1759
1724 Julius Caesar
1725 Rodelinda
1735 Alcina
1738 Xerxes
1744 Semele

PERGOLESI 1710-1736
1752 Serva Padrona

GLUCK 1714-1787
1767 Alceste
1774 Iphigene en Aulide
1779 Iphigenie en Tauride
1762 Orpheus & Euridice

HAYDN 1732-1809
1781 Fedelta Premiata

MOZART 1756 -1791
1781 Idomeneo
1782 Seraglio
1786 Marriage of Figaro
1787 Don Giovanni
1790 Cosi fan Tutte
1791 Clemenza di Tito
1791 Magic Flute

BEETHOVEN 1770 -1827
1805 Fidelio

WEBER 1786 -1826
1821 Freischütz
1823 Euryanthe

MEYERBEER 1791-1864
1836 Huguenots

ROSSINI 1792 -1868
- 1808 Italian Girl in Algiers
- 1816 Barber of Seville
- 1817 Cinderella
- 1823 Semiramide
- 1828 Comte Ory

DONIZETTI 1797-1848
- 1832 Elisir d'Amore
- 1834 Mary Stuart
- 1835 Lucia dI Lammermoor
- 1843 Don Pasquale

BELLINI 1801- 1835
- 1831 Norma
- 1831 Sonnambula

BERLIOZ 1803 -1869
- 1863 Trojans

VERDI 1813 - 1901
- 1842 Nabucco
- 1847 Macbeth
- 1851 Rigoletto
- 1853 Trovatore
- 1857 Simon Boccanegra
- 1857 Traviata
- 1859 Masked Ball
- 1862 Force of Destiny
- 1867 Don Carlos
- 1871 Aida
- 1887 Othello
- 1893 Falstaff

WAGNER 1813 -1883
- 1843 Flying Dutchman
- 1845 Tannhaüser
- 1850 Lohengrin
- 1865 Tristan and Isolde
- 1868 Mastersingers
- 1870 Valkyrie
- 1876 Rhinegold
- 1876 Twilight of the Gods
- 1876 Siegfried
- 1882 Parsifal

GOUNOD 1818 -1893
- 1859 Faust

SMETANA 1824 - 1884
- 1866 Bartered Bride

STRAUSS (*Johann*) 1825 - 1899
- 1874 Fledermaus

BORODIN 1833 -1887
- 1890 Prince Igor

SAINT-SAENS 1835 - 1921
- 1877 Samson and Dalila

BIZET 1838 - 1875
  1875 Carmen

MUSSORGSKY 1839 - 1881
  1874 Boris Godounov

TCHAIKOVSKY 1840 - 1893
  1879 Eugene Onegin
  1890 Queen of Spades

DVORÁK 1841 - 1904
  1901 Rusalka

MASSENET 1842 -1912
  1884 Manon

SULLIVAN 1842 -1900
  1885 Mikado

RIMSKY-KORSAKOV 1844 - 1908
  1882 Snow Maiden
  1910 Golden Cockerel

HUMPERDINCK 1854 - 1921
  1893 Hansel and Gretel

JANAÇEK 1854 - 1928
  1904 Jenufa
  1921 Katya Kabanova
  1924 Cunning Little Vixen
  1926 Makropulos Affair

LEONCAVALLO 1857- 1919
  1892 Pagliacci

PUCCINI 1858 -1924
  1893 Manon Lescaut
  1896 Bohème
  1900 Tosca
  1904 Madam Butterfly
  1910 Girl of the Golden West
  1918 Gianni Schicci
  1918 Sister Angelica
  1918 Tabarro
  1926 Turandot

MASCAGNI 1863 - 1945
  1890 Cavalleria Rusticana

STRAUSS *(Richard)* 1864- *1949*
  1905 Salome
  1909 Elektra
  1911 Rosenkavalier
  1912 Ariadne on Naxos
  1933 Arabella

GIORDANO 1867-1948
1896 Andrea Chenier

VAUGHAN WILLIAMS 1872 -1958
1924 Hugh the Drover

BARTÓK 1881 - 1945
1918 Duke Bluebeard

STRAVINSKY 1882 - 1971
1951 Rake's Progress

BERG 1885 - 1935
1925 Wozzeck
1937 Lulu

PROKOFIEV 1891- 1953
1921 Love for Three Oranges

GERSHWIN 1898 -1937
1935 Porgy and Bess

BERNSTEIN 1918 -1990
1957 Candide

WALTON 1902 -1983
1954 Troilus and Cressida

TIPPETT 1905 -1998
1955 Midsummer Marriage
1962 King Priam

BRITTEN 1913 -1976
1945 Peter Grimes
1947 Albert Herring
1951 Billy Budd
1960 Midsummer Night's Dream

SONDHEIM 1930 -
1979 Sweeney Todd
1987 Into the Woods

GLASS 1937 -
1984 Akhnaten

COMPREHENSIVE INDEX OF OPERAS
(In italics)
AND COMPOSERS
(In **BOLD CAPITALS**)

[Here we miss out the initial *"The, La, Die"* etc. and usually only include accents for the first entry, adopting anglicised forms elsewhere. Works by each composer are listed again after their name.]

Aida 5
Akhnaten 5
Albert Herring 6
Alceste 6
Alcina 7
Andrea Chénier 7
Angelica (Sister) 64
Arabella 8
Ariadne on Naxos 8
Ballo in Maschera 9
Barber of Seville 9
Bartered Bride 10
BARTÓK 1881-1945
* *Duke Bluebeard* 20

BEETHOVEN 1770-1827
* *Fidelio* 24
Beggar's Opera 10
BELLINI 1801-1835
* *Norma* 48
* *Sonnambula* 65
BERG 1885-1935
* *Lulu* 38
* *Wozzeck* 73
BERLIOZ 1803-1869
* *Trojans* 70
BERNSTEIN 1918-1990
* *Candide* 13
Billy Budd 11
BIZET 1838-1875
* *Carmen* 13
Bluebeard (Duke) 20
Boccanegra (Simon) 63
Bohéme 11
Boris Godounov 12
BORODIN 1833-1887
* *Prince Igor* 53
BRITTEN 1913-1976
* *Albert Herring* 6
* *Billy Budd* 11
* *Midsummer Night's Dream* 46
* *Peter Grimes* 52
Budd (Billy) 11
Butterfly (Madam) 39
Caesar (Julius) 33
Calisto 12
Candide 13

87

Carlos (Don) 18
Carmen 13
Cavalleria Rusticana 14
CAVALLI 1602-1676
*   *Calisto 12*
Cenerentola 14
Chénier (Andrea) 7
Cinderella 14
Clemenza di Tito 15
Comte Ory 15
Coronation of Poppea 16
Cosi Fan Tutte 17
Cunning Little Vixen 17
Dido and Aeneas 18
Don Carlos 18
Don Giovanni 19
DONIZETTI 1797-1848
*   *Don Pasquale 19*
*   *Elisir d'Amore 21*
*   *Lucia di Lammermoor 37*
*   *Mary Stuart 43*
Don Pasquale 19
Duke Bluebeard's Castle 20
Dutchman (Flying) 75
DVORÁK 1841-1904
*   *Rusalka 58*
Elektra 20
L'Elisir d'Amore 21
Elixir of Love 21
Entführung aus dem Serail (Seraglio) 61
Eugene Onegin 21

Euryanthe 22
Falstaff 22
Faust 23
Fedelta Premiata 23
Fidelio 24
Figaro's Wedding (Marriage of Figaro) 42
Fledermaus 24
Flying Dutchman 25
Force of Destiny 25
Forza del Destino 25
Freischütz 26
GAY 1685-1732
*   *Beggar's Opera 10*
GERSHWIN 1898-1937
*   *Porgy and Bess 53*
Gianni Schicchi 26
GIORDANO 1867-1948
*   *Andrea Chenier 7*
Giovanni (Don) 19
Girl of the Golden West 27
GLASS 1937-
*   *Akhnaten 5*
GLUCK 1714-1787
*   *Alceste 6*
*   *Iphigenie en Aulide 31*
*   *Iphigenie en Tauride 31*
*   *Orpheus & Euridice 50*
Golden Cockerel 27
Götterdämmerung (Twilight of the Gods) 72

GOUNOD 1818-1893
*   Faust 23
Grimes (Peter) 52
HANDEL 1685-1759
*   Alcina 7
*   Julius Caesar 33
*   Rodelinda 57
*   Semele 60
*   Xerxes 74
Hänsel and Gretel 28
HAYDN 1732-1809
*   Fedelta Premiata 23
Herring (Albert) 6
**HUMPERDINCK 1854-
                1921**
*   Hansel and Gretel 28
Hugh the Drover 28
Huguenots 29
Idomeneo 29
Incoronazione di Poppea
                                  16
Into the Woods 30
Iphigénie en Aulide 31
Iphigénie en Tauride 31
Italian Girl in Algiers 32
Italiana in Algeri 32
JANÁČEK 1854-1928
*   Cunning Little Vixen 17
*   Jenufa 32
*   Katya Kabanova 34
*   Makropulos Affair 40
Jenufa 32

Julius Caesar 33
Kát'a Kabanová 34
Katya Kabanova 34
King Priam 34
Lady Macbeth of Mtsensk
     35
**LEONCAVALLO 1857-
                1919**
*   Pagliacci 51
Lohengrin 36
Love for Three Oranges 36
Lucia di Lammermoor 37
Lulu 38
Macbeth (Shostakovich) 35
Macbeth (Verdi) 39
Madam Butterfly 39
Magic Flute 40
Makropulos Affair 40
Manon (Massenet) 41
Manon Lescaut (Puccini) 42
Maria Stuarda 43
Marriage of Figaro 42
Mary Stuart 43
MASCAGNI 1863-1945
*   Cavalleria Rusticana 14
Masked Ball 44
MASSENET 1842-1912
 *   Manon 41
Mastersingers 44
Meistersinger von Nürnberg
     44
Merry Wives of Windsor 45

89

MEYERBEER 1791-1864
* Huguenots 29
Midsummer Marriage 45
Midsummer Night's
                  Dream 46
Mikado 47
MONTEVERDI 1567-1643
* Coronation of Poppea
                        16
* Orfeo 49
* Ritorno D'Ulisse
                 In Patria 57
MOZART 1756-1791
* Clemenza di Tito 15
* Cosi fan Tutte 17
* Don Giovanni 19
* Idomeneo 29
* Magic Flute 40
* Marriage of Figaro 42
* Seraglio 61
MUSSORGSKY 1839-1881
* Boris Godounov 12
Nabucco 48
NICOLAI 1810 - 1849
* Merry Wives of Windsor
                        45
Norma 48
Nozze di Figaro 42
Onegin (Eugene) 21
Orfeo 49
Orfeo ed Euridice 50
Orpheus and Euridice 50
Otello 50

Othello 50
Pagliacci 51
Parsifal 51
Pasquale (Don) 19
Pelléas and Mélisande 52
PERGOLESI 1710-1736
* Serva Padrona 62
Peter Grimes 52
Poppea 16
Porgy and Bess 53
Priam (King) 34
Prince Igor 53
PROKOFIEV 1891-1953
* Love for Three
                 Oranges 36
PUCCINI 1858-1924
* Bohème 11
* Gianni Schicci 26
* Girl of the
            Golden West 27
* Madam Butterfly 3
* Manon Lescaut 42
* Sister Angelica 64
* Tabarro 67
* Tosca 68
* Turandot 71
PURCELL 1659-1695
* Dido and Aeneas 18
Queen of Spades 54
Rake's Progress 54
Rhinegold 55
Rheingold 55
Rigoletto 56

**RIMSKY-KORSAKOV
               1844-1908**
*   Golden Cockerel 27
*   Snow Maiden 64
Ring 56
Ring of the Nibelung 56
Ritorno d'Ulisse in Patria
                              57
Rodelinda 57
Rosenkavalier 58
ROSSINI 1792-1868
*   Barber of Seville 9
*   Cinderella 14
*   Comte Ory 15
*   Italian Girl in Algiers
                              32
*   Semiramide 61
Rusalka 58
SAINT-SAËNS 1835-1921
*   Samson and Dalila 60
Salome 59
Samson and Dalila 60
Schicci (Gianni) 26
Semele 60
Semiramide 61
Seraglio 61
Serva Padrona 62
Seville (Barber of) 9
**SHOSTAKOVICH
               1906-1975**
*   Lady Macbeth of
          Mtsensk   35
Siegfried 62

Simon Boccanegra 63
Sister Angelica 64
SMETANA 1824-1884
*   Bartered Bride 10
Snow Maiden 64
SONDHEIM 1930-
*   Into the Woods 30
*   Sweeney Todd 66
Sonnambula 65
**STRAUSS *(Johann)*
              *1825-1899***
*   Fledermaus 24
**STRAUSS *(Richard)*
              *1864-1949***
*   Arabella 8
*   Ariadne on Naxos 8
*   Elektra 20
*   Rosenkavalier 58
*   Salome 59
STRAVINSKY 1882-1971
*   Rake's Progress 54
SULLIVAN 1842-1900
*   Mikado 47
Sweeney Todd 66
Tabarro 67
Tannhäuser 67
TCHAIKOVSKY 1840-1893
*   Eugene Onegin 21
*   Queen of Spades 54
TIPPETT 1905-1998
*   King Priam 34
*   Midsummer
            Marriage 45

91

Tito (Clemenza di) 15
Tosca 68
Traviata 68
Tristan and Isolde 69
Troilus and Cressida 69
Trojans 70
Trovatore 70
Troyens 70
Turandot 71
Twilight of the Gods 72
Valkyrie 72
VAUGHAN WILLIAMS 1872-1958
* *Hugh the Drover* 28

VERDI 1813-1901
* *Aida* 5
* *Don Carlos* 18
* *Falstaff* 22
* *Force of Destiny* 25
* *Macbeth* 39
* *Masked Ball* 44
* *Nabucco* 48
* *Othello* 50
* *Rigoletto* 56
* *Simon Boccanegra* 63
* *Traviata* 68
* *Trovatore* 70

Vixen (Cunning Little) 17

WAGNER 1813-1901
* *Flying Dutchman* 25
* *Lohengrin* 36
* *Mastersingers* 44
* *Parsifal* 51
* *Rhinegold* 55
* *Ring (of Nibelung)* 56
* *Siegfried* 62
* *Tannhäuser* 67
* *Tristan and Isolde* 69
* *Twilight of the Gods* 72
* *Valkyrie* 72

WALTON 1002-1983
* *Troilus and Cressida* 69

WEBER 1786-1826
* *Euryanthe* 22
* *Freischutz* 26

Wozzeck 73
Xerxes 74
Zauberflöte (Magic Flute) 40